So many more knock knock jokes to make your friends and family laugh and groan!

AGES 5+

ISBN 978-1-926677-97-2
50699
9781926677972

$6.99

Printed in China

KNOCK KNOCK JOKES

BUG BRAINS

NICKY BIRD

FOLK LORE PUBLISHING

Knock knock.
Who's there?
Oily.
Oily who?
The Oily bird catches the worm!
Knock knock.
Who's there?
Adolf.
Adolf who?
Adolf ball hit me in the mouth.

Knock knock.
Who's there?
Noise.
Noise who?
Noise to see you.
Knock knock.
Who's there?
Urinal.
Urinal who?
Urinal-ot of trouble.

Knock knock.
Who's there?
Abyssinia.
Abyssinia who?
Abyssinia when I get back.
Knock knock.
Who's there?
Voodoo.
Voodoo who?
Voodoo you think you are?

Knock knock.
Who's there?
Yukon.
Yukon who?
Yukon go away and come back later.
Knock knock.
Who's there?
Bed.
Bed who?
Bed you can't guess who I am.

Knock knock.
Who's there?
Renata.
Renata who?
Renata milk. Can I borrow some?
Knock knock.
Who's there?
Salome.
Salome who?
Salome and cheese sandwich, please.

Knock knock.
Who's there?
Mavis.
Mavis who?
Mavis be the last time I knock on this door.
Knock knock.
Who's there?
Carrie.
Carrie who?
Carrie me home. I'm tired.

Knock knock.
Who's there?
Lego.
Lego who?
Lego of me, and I'll tell you.
Knock knock.
Who's there?
Dennis.
Dennis who?
Dennis says I need to have a tooth out.

Knock knock.
Who's there?
Pasta.
Pasta who?
Pasta salt please.
Knock knock.
Who's there?
Seymour.
Seymour who?
You'll Seymour if you look out of the window.

Knock knock.
Who's there?
Matthew.
Matthew who?
Matthew lace has come undone.
Knock knock.
Who's there?
Norma Lee.
Norma Lee who?
Norma Lee I don't go round knocking on doors.

Knock knock.
Who's there?
Eliza.
Eliza who?
Eliza wake at night thinking up new jokes.
Knock knock.
Who's there?
Thea.
Thea who?
Thea later, alligator.

Knock knock.
Who's there?
Oil.
Oil who?
Oil be seeing you soon.
Knock knock.
Who's there?
Adore.
Adore who?
Adore stands between us. Open up!

Knock knock.
Who's there?
Guitar.
Guitar who?
Guitar coats. It's raining hard.
Knock knock.
Who's there?
Pasture.
Pasture who?
Pasture bedtime, isn't it?

Knock knock.
Who's there?
Rhoda.
Rhoda who?
Rhoda boat as fast as you can.
Knock knock.
Who's there?
Cat.
Cat who?
Cat you understand what I'm saying?

Knock knock.
Who's there?
Beezer.
Beezer who?
Beezer black and yellow and make honey.
Knock knock.
Who's there?
Flea.
Flea who?
Flea blind mice.

Knock knock.
Who's there?
Ella.
Ella who?
Ella-mentary, my dear Watson.
Knock knock.
Who's there?
Dewey.
Dewey who?
Dewey have to keep telling these silly jokes?

Knock knock.
Who's there?
Jez.
Jez who?
Jez a minute.
Knock knock.
Who's there?
Forbes.
Forbes who?
May the Forbes be with you.

Knock knock.
Who's there?
Megan.
Megan who?
Megan a cake. Do you want a piece?
Knock knock.
Who's there?
CD.
CD who?
CD person on your doorstep? It's me.

Knock knock.
Who's there?
Iguana.
Iguana who?
Iguana hold your hand.
Knock knock.
Who's there?
Harmony.
Harmony who?
Harmony knock knock jokes do you expect me to know?

Knock knock.
Who's there?
Gwen.
Gwen who?
Gwen will I see you again?
Knock knock.
Who's there?
Nose.
Nose who?
I nose plenty more knock knock jokes. Don't worry.

Knock knock.
Who's there?
Sara.
Sara who?
Sara 'nother way in?
Knock knock.
Who's there?
Theodore.
Theodore who?
Theodore is shut. Please open it.

Knock knock.
Who's there?
Hannah.
Hannah who?
Hannah partridge in a pear tree.
Knock knock.
Who's there?
Viper.
Viper who?
Viper your nose. It's running.

Knock knock.
Who's there?
Patrick.
Patrick who?
Patrick-ed me into coming.
Knock knock.
Who's there?
Sherlock.
Sherlock who?
Sherlock your door. Someone could break in.

Knock knock.
Who's there?
Wanda.
Wanda who?
Wanda off, and you'll get lost.
Knock knock.
Who's there?
Alfred.
Alfred who?
Who's Alfred of the Big Bad Wolf?

Knock knock.
Who's there?
Rita.
Rita who?
Rita good book, and you might learn something.
Knock knock.
Who's there?
Thermos.
Thermos who?
Thermos be a better knock knock joke than this one.

Knock knock.
Who's there?
Utah.
Utah who?
Utah me to knock.
Knock knock.
Who's there?
Chicken.
Chicken who?
Chicken the oven! I smell something burning!

Knock knock.
Who's there?
Diana.
Diana who?
I'm Diana thirst. Can I have some water, please?
Knock knock.
Who's there?
Jim.
Jim who?
Jim mind if we come in?

Knock knock.
Who's there?
Ike.
Ike who?
Ike-n't stop laughing.
Knock knock.
Who's there?
Essen.
Essen who?
Essen it fun to listen to these jokes?

Knock knock.
Who's there?
Olive.
Olive who?
Olive you.
Knock knock.
Who's there?
Sharon.
Sharon who?
Sharon share alike.

Knock knock.
Who's there?
Leif.
Leif who?
Leif me alone, and stop asking all these questions!
Knock knock.
Who's there?
Kenya.
Kenya who?
Kenya guess who it is?

Knock knock.
Who's there?
Belize.
Belize who?
Belize in yourself.
Knock knock.
Who's there?
Francis.
Francis who?
Francis where people speak French.

Knock knock.
Who's there?
Warner.
Warner who?
Warner lift? My car's outside.
Knock knock.
Who's there?
Olga.
Olga who?
Olga home if you don't open up.

Knock knock.
Who's there?
Shoes.
Shoes who?
Shoes me, I didn't mean to bump into you.
Knock knock.
Who's there?
Missouri.
Missouri who?
Missouri loves company.

Knock knock.
Who’s there?
Patsy.
Patsy who?
Patsy dog on the head. He likes it.
Knock knock.
Who’s there?
Harp.
Harp who?
Harp, the Herald Angels Sing.

Knock knock.
Who's there?
Me.
Me who?
I didn't know you had a cat.
Knock knock.
Who's there?
Robin.
Robin who?
Someone's Robin your house!

Knock knock.
Who's there?
Betty.
Betty who?
It's Betty-bye time.
Knock knock.
Who's there?
Aida.
Aida who?
Aida huge breakfast before going to school.

Knock knock.
Who's there?
Sherwood.
Sherwood who?
Sherwood like to come in.
Knock knock.
Who's there?
India.
India who?
India nighttime I go to sleep.

Knock knock.
Who's there?
Joan.
Joan who?
Joan you remember me?
Knock knock.
Who's there?
Thumb.
Thumb who?
Thumb like it hot, and thumb like it cold.

Knock knock.
Who's there?
Twig.
Twig who?
Twig or tweat!
Knock knock.
Who's there?
Vlad.
Vlad who?
Vlad to meet you.

Knock knock.
Who's there?
Virtue.
Virtue who?
Virtue get all these great jokes?
Knock knock.
Who's there?
Ketchup.
Ketchup who?
Ketchup with me, and I'll tell you.

Knock knock.
Who's there?
Ahmed.
Ahmed who?
Ahmed a big mistake coming here.
Knock knock.
Who's there?
Lenny.
Lenny who?
Lenny in, I'm hungry.

Knock knock.
Who's there?
Mikey.
Mikey who?
Mikey won't fit in this lock.
Knock knock.
Who's there?
Nuisance.
Nuisance who?
What's nuisance since yesterday?

Knock knock.
Who's there?
Annie.
Annie who?
Annie thing you can do, I can do better.
Knock knock.
Who's there?
Ben and Anna.
Ben and Anna who?
Ben and Anna split.

Knock knock.
Who's there?
Catskills.
Catskills who?
Catskills mice.
Knock knock.
Who's there?
Leonie.
Leonie who?
You're Leonie
one I love.

Knock knock.
Who's there?
Mice.
Mice who?
Mice to meet you.
Knock knock.
Who's there?
Diploma.
Diploma who?
Diploma will come and fix the leaky faucet.

Knock knock.
Who's there?
Nurse.
Nurse who?
There's nurse sense talking to you.
Knock knock.
Who's there?
Midas.
Midas who?
Midas well have stayed at home since you won't open the door.

Knock knock.
Who's there?
Howie.
Howie who?
I'm fine. How are you?
Knock knock.
Who's there?
Boo.
Boo who?
Well, you don't have to cry about it.

Knock knock.
Who's there?
Sloane.
Sloane who?
Sloane-ly outside. Let me in.
Knock knock.
Who's there?
Sadie.
Sadie who?
Sadie magic word, and I'll disappear!

Knock knock.
Who's there?
Foster.
Foster who?
He's Foster than a speeding bullet.
Knock knock.
Who's there?
Pecan.
Pecan who?
Pecan somebody your own size!

Knock knock.
Who's there?
Harold.
Harold who?
Harold do you think I am?
Knock knock.
Who's there?
Iona.
Iona who?
Iona a house, a car and a dog.

Knock knock.
Who's there?
Knock knock.
Who's there?
Knock knock!
I'm sorry, but my mother doesn't allow me to speak to strangers.
Knock knock.
Who's there?
Dismay.
Dismay who?
Dismay surprise you, but I have a lot more jokes.

Knock knock.
Who's there?
Lee.
Lee who?
Lee me alone.
Knock knock.
Who's there?
Alison.
Alison who?
Alison to you
if you listen to me.

Knock knock.
Who's there?
Rockies.
Rockies who?
Rockies my favourite type of music.
Knock knock.
Who's there?
Harris.
Harris who?
Harris nice to have on the top of your head.

Knock knock.
Who's there?
Elsie.
Elsie who?
Elsie you later.
Knock knock.
Who's there?
Thistle.
Thistle who?
Thistle be the last time I knock on this door!

Knock knock.
Who's there?
Arfur.
Arfur who?
Arfur got!
Knock knock.
Who's there?
Abby.
Abby who?
Abby birthday to you!

Knock knock.
Who's there?
Olivia.
Olivia who?
Olivia me alone.
Knock knock.
Who's there?
Iran.
Iran who?
Iran away when you answered before.

Knock knock.
Who's there?
Banana.
Banana who?
Knock knock.
Who's there?
Banana.
Banana who?
Knock knock.
Who's there?
Banana.
Banana who?
Knock knock.
Who's there?
Orange.
Orange who?
Orange you glad I didn't say "Banana"?

Knock knock.
Who's there?
Frank.
Frank who?
Frankenstein.
Knock knock.
Who's there?
Watson.
Watson who?
Watson the menu today? I'm hungry.

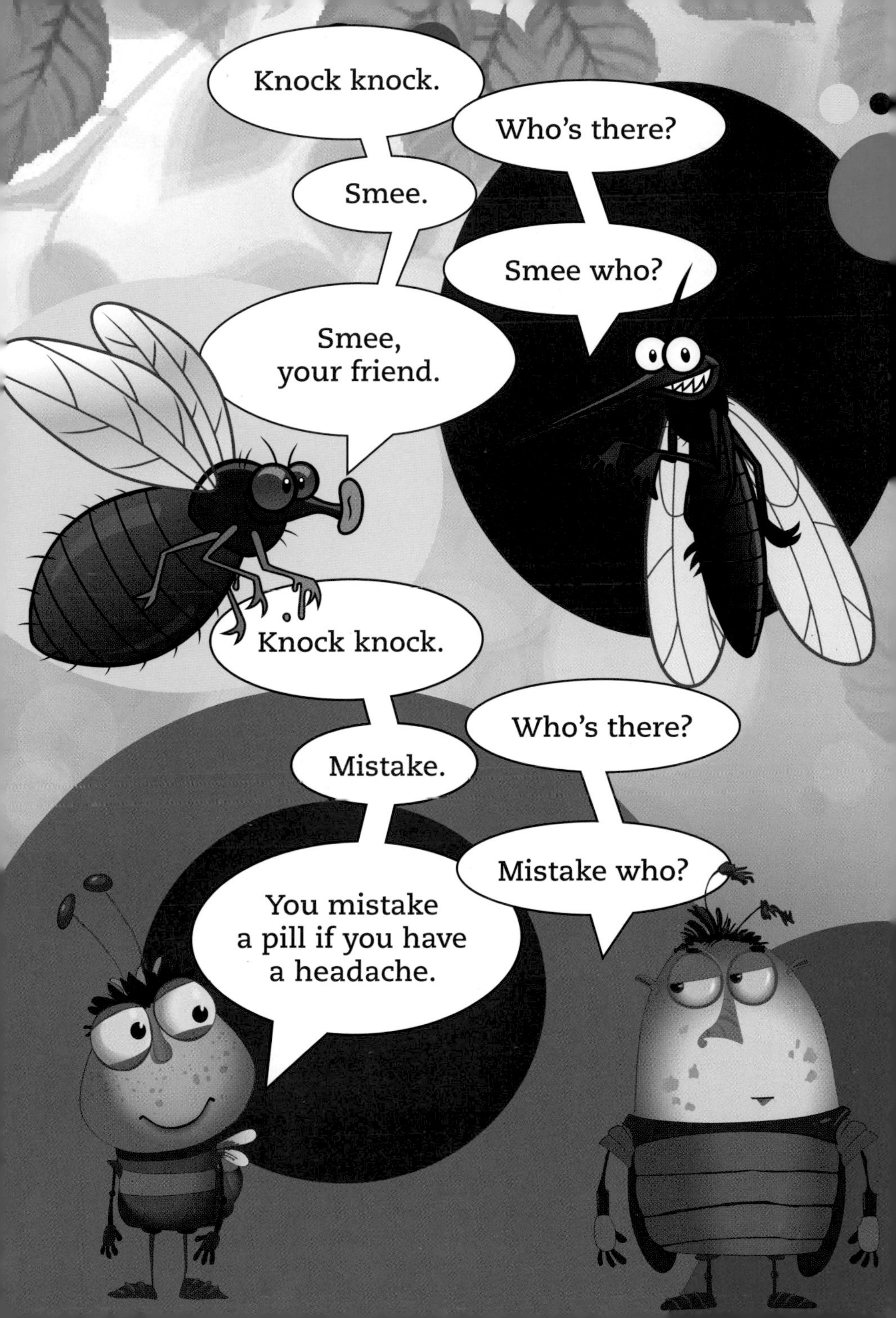
Knock knock.
Who's there?
Smee.
Smee who?
Smee, your friend.
Knock knock.
Who's there?
Mistake.
Mistake who?
You mistake a pill if you have a headache.

Knock knock.
Who's there?
Juicy.
Juicy who?
Juicy what I just saw?
Knock knock.
Who's there?
Kojak.
Kojak who?
Kojak up the car. I've got a flat tire.

Knock knock.
Who's there?
Al.
Al who?
Al be seeing you.
Knock knock.
Who's there?
Bolivia.
Bolivia who?
Boliva me,
I know what I'm
talking about.

Knock knock.
Who's there?
Lettuce.
Lettuce who?
Lettuce in, and I'll tell you.
Knock knock.
Who's there?
Albert.
Albert who?
Albert you can't guess who this is.

Knock knock.
Who's there?
Closure.
Closure who?
Closure mouth when you eat.
Knock knock.
Who's there?
Sofa.
Sofa who?
Sofa, so good.

First printed in 2015 10 9 8 7 6 5 4 3 2 1

Printed in China

The Publisher: Folklore Publishing Ltd.
Website: www.folklorepublishing.com

Library and Archives Canada Cataloguing in Publication

Bird, Nicky, 1961–, author

Knock knock jokes : bug brains / Nicky Bird.

ISBN 978-1-926677-97-2 (paperback)

1. Knock-knock jokes. 2. Wit and humor, Juvenile. I. Title.

PN6231.K55B573 2016 jC818'.602 C2015-907834-2

Cover images: Front cover: Thinkstock: cthoman; Refluo. *Back cover:* Thinkstock: Hemera; ridjam; sababaJJ; Sergey Markov.

Background images: Thinkstock: Aliaksandr, 2–3, 12–13, 24, 36–37, 48–49, 60–61; Dynamic Graphics 2007, 10–11, 20–21, 34–35, 44–45, 56–57; ok-sana, 4–5, 14–15, 26–27, 38–39, 50–51, 62–63; rvika, 6–7, 16–17, 22–23, 28–29, 32–33, 40–41, 46–47, 52–53, 58.

Image credits: Thinkstock: Alexey Bannykh, 2, 4, 9, 12, 16, 18, 29, 30–32, 38, 42–45, 47, 54, 58, 62; artnimals, 6, 20, 51; ChrisGorgio, 4–7, 10, 11, 15, 19, 21, 24–26, 36–38, 47–50; cthoman, 3, 8, 12, 17, 23, 30, 32, 40, 43, 55, 57, 62; losiks, 7, 13, 19, 21, 33, 39, 42, 46, 50, 59, 63; MimaCZ, 5, 14, 27, 35, 52, 56, 60; nyamol, 7, 10, 13, 21, 22, 25, 33, 37, 41, 42, 49, 50, 63; refluo, 3, 4, 6, 8, 10, 12, 14, 15, 17, 18, 20, 22, 23, 25, 26, 29, 30, 32, 34–36, 39–41, 43, 44, 46, 48, 51, 53, 55, 57, 59–62;ridjam; 2, 8, 14, 16, 28, 31, 34, 45, 54, 60; sababaJJ, 5, 9, 11, 19, 24, 27, 36, 38, 47, 48, 52, 56, 58; Sergey Markov: 5, 10, 22, 25, 27, 37, 41, 43, 48, 49, 52, 56; Tigatelu, 2–6, 8, 9, 11, 13–17, 19, 20, 22–24, 26–29, 31, 33–37, 40, 41, 44, 45, 49, 51–55, 59–61, 63; Val_Iva, 8, 9, 18, 30, 31, 42, 43, 54, 55.

Produced with the assistance of the Government of Alberta, Alberta Media Fund.

Alberta Government

We acknowledge the financial support of the Government of Canada through the Canada Book Fund (CBF) for our publishing activities.

Canadian Heritage Patrimoine canadien

PC: 30